CW00459993

Dedicated to the love between siblings around the world.

Text Copyright © 2021 by Karishma Motiram
Illustrations Copyright © 2021 by Seema Khatri

All rights reserved. No part of this publication may be reproduced, stored or introduced into a retrieval system, or transmitted, in any form, or by any means (electronic, mechanical, photocopying, recording or otherwise) without the prior permission of the authors.

Any person who does any unauthorised act in relation to this publication may be liable to criminal prosecution and civil claims for damages.

Adventures with Teddy
Raksha Bandhan

With their **warm**, **cosy blankets**, and *favourite books*, Leena and Dhru were ready for bed.

Just before Mum turned the lights off, they noticed Indian clothes hanging on their wardrobe handles.

"What are those for, Mum?" asked Dhru.

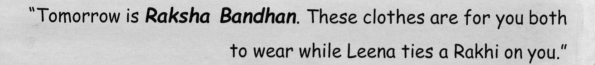

"Tomorrow is **Raksha Bandhan**. These clothes are for you both to wear while Leena ties a Rakhi on you."

"Is that when I tie the string on Dhru?"

Mum smiled, "That's right. Goodnight you two, time to go to sleep now. Don't read for too long., we have an early start!" reminded Mum, as she switched off the lights.

"*Leena....?*" Whispered Dhru. "Can I ask you a question?"

Leena closed her book and replied, "o*f course you can*, what's up?"

"Why do you tie a Rakhi on me?" he asked.

"I don't know why, but I know how we can find out…"
she said, as a playful smile spread across her face.

"REALLY? Right now!?" said Dhru, leaping out of bed.

They both grabbed Teddy, pressed his magic watch and got ready for an adventure to learn **all** about Raksha Bandhan.

The room transformed, with wind

Swirling around them

Off they went onto a **fun adventure!**

As quick a flash they transported into a town that looked like something they had never seen before...

"Teddy, **where are we?**" they asked.

"This looks like **the olden days**" said Leena, with a curious look on her face.

"That's because we've travelled back in time. Look behind you!" said Teddy.

Dhru jumped up and down pointing towards a palace. "Woah, can we go in there? Please?" Teddy chuckled at Dhru's excitement.

"That's

exactly

where

we're

going!

This palace is in India and it belongs to King Bali. It is being protected by Lord Vishnu, because he made a promise to guard it, but that means he is living *faaar* away from his wife, Goddess Lakshmi. She has really been missing him."

"But what does that have to do with Raksha Bandhan?" asked Leena.

"Come with me to find out..." said Teddy.

Dhru squealed with delight and squeezed Leena's hand, as Teddy led the way.

They walked through the beautiful palace and onto a terrace, where they stopped to watch what was happening.

"See that young woman? That's **Goddess Lakshmi**," explained Teddy.

"Goddess Lakshmi has travelled a *very very long way* and she has been living in the palace, secretly disguised as a *Brahmin* who needs shelter."

She has waited until *Shravana Purnima*, which is when there is a **full moon**. On this special day, she is tying a cotton Rakhi on King Bali's wrist."

As Leena and Dhru watched wide-eyed, Teddy continued explaining.

"The King is touched by the kindness of her tying a Rakhi and asks what she would like as a 'thank you gift'. Goddess Lakshmi is now explaining who she really is, and asks the King to free Lord Vishnu of his promise, so he can come home to her.

This is the only gift she wants... for her husband to come home."

"Woah..." both Leena and Dhru are speechless.

"King Bali then asked them to promise they would come to visit and share a meal with him at the palace, every year on this special day.

This is why sisters traditionally go to their brother's house, to tie a Rakhi."

"When you're older would you travel that far to tie a Rakhi on me?"
interrupted Dhru. Leena chuckled and gave him a big hug.

"Teddy…" Leena continued, "I thought you tie a Rakhi on your brother.
Was King Bali her brother?" she asked.

"He was **not** her brother... well spotted!" replied Teddy.

"The stories from history show that when a girl ties a Rakhi around the wrist of a boy, they form a bond *like a brother and sister*, and it becomes his duty to look after her."

Teddy quietly led the children back out of the palace, as a BIG smile grew on Dhru's face.

"So even though I'm little and Leena is older, the Rakhi gives ME the power to look after HER?" he asked.

"Actually, sisters do look after their brothers. Let's take another trip and I'll show you what I mean," said Teddy.

"Hold on tight!"

"**Hey**!" exclaimed Leena. "How come we can't look after our brothers?"

BUMP, they landed in a small village.

"What's happening here?"
asked Dhru.

"This is a sister tying a Rakhi on her brother, many years ago. You see, the Rakhi is a prayer in a cotton thread. When the sister ties this, she is **protecting her brother through a prayer.**"

"Cool, so I walk around with a prayer on my hand?" wondered Dhru. "Waaiiit a minute. That's not fair, how come he doesn't pray for me?" questioned Leena.

They took a seat, while Teddy answered Leena's question.

"In the olden days, boys and girls had very different roles. So by tying the Rakhi, they are looking after each other in the only way they knew how."

"So sisters would pray for God to protect their brothers. Then the brothers would promise to look after their sisters as thank you?" asked Leena, in confusion.

"That's right! In fact, the word 'raksha' means 'to protect,' and the word 'bandhan' means 'bond'," replied Teddy.

"COOL!" shouted Leena and Dhru.

Teddy's watch began to beep, which meant it was time to go home and get some rest!

Off they went...
back to their cosy beds!

The next morning...

"Happy Raksha Bandhan!" exclaimed Leena and Dhru.

They were **so** excited that they jumped out of bed, brushed, bathed and got changed into the clothes Mum had left out the night before.

They went down to the kitchen for breakfast, ready for an awesome day!

"Up and ready?" asked Mum, surprised that they were already dressed up!

"Can I tie my Rakhi on Dhru right now, Mum? **Pleeease**?"

"WOW, you're very excited! Are you sure you don't want to wait until later?" she asked.

"**WE'RE SURE!** They cried together. "Okay then..." agreed Mum.

Mum and Leena gathered the Rakhi, some sweets, *kanku and chokha* in a beautiful tray.

Leena began by putting a *chandlo* on Dhru. Then, she carefully tied the Rakhi on him and fed him something sweet.

"Seeing you two right now reminds me of *Mama* and I when we were younger. Maybe this year I will call him over and ask him to spend the day here for *Raksha Bandhan*."

"You can't do that!" exclaimed Dhru.

"You're supposed to go to Mama's house just like Lakshmi went to King Bali." explained Leena.

Mum **stared at them** in amazement and wondered... now, where could have learned that from?

"Gotta love Teddy!"
They thought to themselves,
as another adventure comes to an end.

We hope you enjoyed learning about Raksha Bandhan!

Hindu traditions go back thousands of years, and over time some of these traditions have changed, developed and even modernized.

Check out these fun facts about Raksha Bandhan:

- ❖ It is said that the 'blessings' in a Rakhi last one year, which is why the festival happens every year.

- ❖ Traditionally, a Rakhi is made of gold and red thread, but today there are new modern threads with gems and many colours.

- ❖ There are many stories about Draupadi tying a Rakhi on Lord Krishna, although historians have questioned if their story is related to Raksha Bandhan.

- ❖ In India, many girls without a brother tie a Rakhi on Lord Krishna.

- ❖ Today, the festival has changed and many people tie a Rakhi, even if they do not hold a brother and sister bond. For example, Priests tie- on devotees, people tie on soldiers, aunties tie on nieces and nephews and many women tie on the Indian Prime Minister too.

Glossary:

'Raksha' – To protect

'Bandhan' – Bond/Tie

'Mama' – Uncle (specifically, your mother's brother)

'Chokha' - Rice

"Kanku" – Also known as Kum Kum. It is a red auspicious powder often used during religious ceremonies, to make a *chandlo*.

"Chandlo" – Also known as "Tilak," is a mark normally made on the forehead.

"Brahmin" – This is the highest caste in the Hindu caste system.

"Shravana Purnima" – One of the most auspicious day on the Hindu calendar.

"King Bali" – Grandson of Prahlada, who was a Vishnu devotee.

ACTIVITIES

On the next page you can draw or stick a photo of you and the person you tie a Rakhi on.

You can even get creative and follow the instructions on how to make your own Rakhi at home!

Happy Raksha Bandhan!

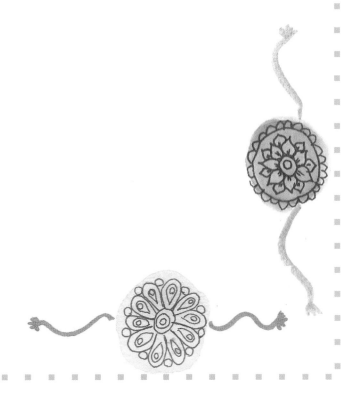

Make your own Rakhi!

Things you'll need

Glue
3 x Colourful foam sheets
Colourful string
Gems or stickers (or both!)

Instructions	Photo Steps
1. Cut a circle (or any shape you like) in 3 different sizes from the colourful foam. *Be sure to make each colour a different size.*	
2. Glue them on top of each other, so the largest shape is at the bottom and the smaller shape is at the top.	
3. Using colourful stickers or gems, decorate the foam with any design you want.	
4. Glue the decorated foam on top of a colourful string.	

Printed in Great Britain
by Amazon

64327443R00020